Best regards!

Gretchen E. Hardy

May 2012

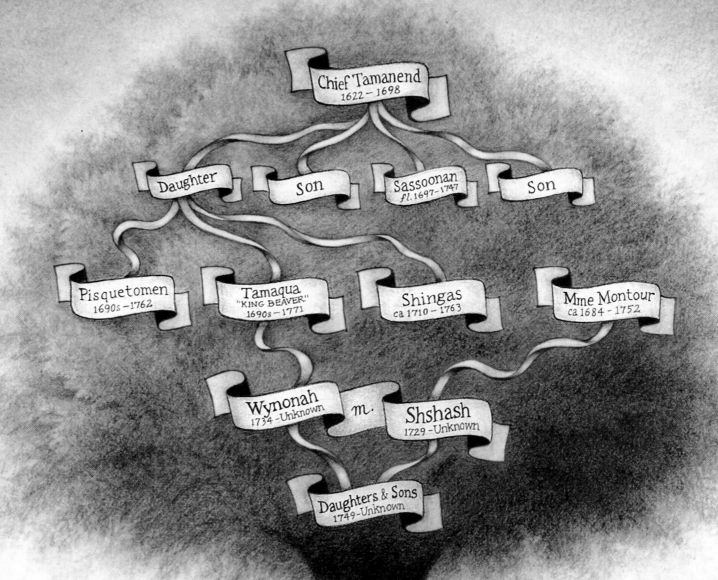

She

If your mother's mother's, ten times mother

    tenderly plaited her toddler's curls, it was with your hand.

You picked that sun-ripened berry; she tasted the sweetness on your tongue.

Two eyes times hundreds, times hundreds

    have looked for the moon's dappled lake reflection.

Laughter chorusing over miles and generations.

Sharing secrets, pain, joy, bloodlines in one kaleidoscopic spirit.

Your mother's mother's, ten times mother's precious legacy.

Daughter.

"Sunshine streamed through the mullioned windows in the log cabin. Mother looked out over Lake Wynonah's diamond sparkle. She felt the glow of inner contentment.

In 1970, a dam had been built across Plum Creek. Water filled the valley with pristine beauty. The lake was named after Wynonah, a remarkable Lenape Delaware woman."

Epilogue

Library Cataloging Data
Hardy, Gretchen Elizabeth Kormanik 1948 -
Kligge, Zoungy 1976 -
  Buttons & Beads
  Lenape Princess Wynonah and the Future President

Summary: Explores role of American Indian women
through the story of Wynonah, a Lenape Delaware.

French and Indian War 1754-1763.

George Washington parallel storyline.

Historical fiction.

Published by Hardy Communications.
2034 Wynonah Dr., Auburn, PA 17922, U.S.A.

Printed in the United States of America.
First edition.

**For the incredible women whose lineage we share:
those who came before us, those who live now,
and those yet to be born.**

Rose Ann, Elizansty, Roberta, Ivy, Agnes, Geraldine, Barbara,
Bettye Jo, Annette, Bridget, Olivia, Charlotte

and

Mai, Elizabeth, Caroline

ISBN 978-0-615-45511-2

BUTTONS & BEADS

LENAPE PRINCESS WYNONAH and THE FUTURE PRESIDENT

Hardy Communications
Auburn, Pennsylvania

What's In A Name?
This book uses tribal names when known and the terms American Indian or Indian. Research and interviews revealed a visceral dislike of the "Native American" nomenclature that has been assigned as "politically correct" to descendants of indigenous peoples.

Author's Note

The voice of historic American Indian women has long been too silent. Imagine the stories they could tell, the lessons they could teach, and the richness they could add as we search for our roots. Let us take what we know of these intrepid female ancestors and, through historical fiction, weave them into one Lenape (Leh-NAH-pay) woman who will be their collective voice. Her essence is validated in the historic deeds and actions of all her native Sisters.

Titled "Princess" by the English, Wynonah was born in 1734 into the Lenape Delaware Royal Family. Where did she live, what did she look like, what did she wear? What did she think? Was she intelligent, wise and strong? How did she mother? How big of a part did she play in her tribe and in history? Imagine her role at this pivotal time in our nation's beginning. Trace her steps from the banks of Pennsylvania's rivers to the Ohio Country. Ride with Wynonah and George Washington to an American Indian campsite on the Schuylkill River.

We do not know where Wynonah spent her final years or how long she lived. Her actions as a vital Lenape Princess impacted the life of a young soldier who would go on to lead a great nation. Enjoy this imaginary walk in her moccasins.

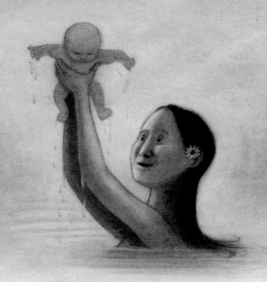

Cold river water engulfed the naked baby, Wynonah. Mother's hands girdled the tiny waist, lifting the infant free. Water dunks in streams or lakes were thought to strengthen a child's ability to grow strong and fight illness. Wails of protest quieted when a leather diaper, padded with cattail fluff, was in place. Wynonah suckled at Mother's breast.

As a child, Wynonah would crouch with Mother in a steamy sweat lodge where water had been poured onto hot rocks. Pores opened to purify body and soul. The pair would then dash with loud whoops into a nearby stream or lake.

Born in 1734 into what the English called the Lenape Delaware Royal Family, Wynonah spent her childhood along the Susquehanna River in Shamokin. Her father, Tamaqua, was the grandson of the great Delaware Chief Tamanend who signed the Treaty of Friendship in 1682 with *Brother Onas* William Penn under the Great Elm at Shackamaxon near Philadelphia.

Tamaqua had many sons, but his only daughter was named Wynonah, which means *first born*. She adored Brothers and loved to throw spears through rolling grapevine hoops with them to hone her hunting skills.

Sometimes Brothers took her to trap beaver. Hunting was even more thrilling. First a prayer was said asking animal spirits permission to hunt. A tobacco gift was placed on the forest floor. With wind toward their faces, they would stalk northern ridges where Father Sun had yet to dry the soft ground. Moccasins were silent carriers. Travel was deliberate, bodies close to the ground. Sunrise, when animals sought food and water, was best. Use of a bow was not a test of strength, but one of skill. "Hunt with your mind," counseled Brothers.

Gutted animals were hung from a tree. Brother would thrust his fist between muscle and hide to work the pelt free. No part of the animal was wasted. Skins were used for clothing, shelter and carriers. Utensils and tools were made from bones. Fat was stored. Intestines were cleaned to stuff with meat. Teeth and claws were crafted into jewelry.

At meals, Wynonah sat with her family on woven mats and ate from pots of food placed on the ground. Tamaqua watched his daughter use a spoon he had carved from mountain laurel. She beamed as pea soup disappeared from her clay bowl. Mother added blueberry juice to their usual water drink.

Duck, bird and goose feathers were plucked and bundled for transport down the Susquehanna to a trading post in Paxtang (Harrisburg) owned by John and Esther Sey Harris. Larger feathers were saved by Lenape women for hair decoration or to weave capes and blankets.

Wynonah watched Mother trade with the proprietress. "These will make fine English comforters," commented Esther as she ran her hand down the side of the bundles. The Lenape mother and daughter paddled home with a bartered brass kettle, a looking glass, and wool cloth.

Evenings often found family members gathered around a fire to sing and tell stories. Wynonah watched her Great-uncle Chief Sassoonan dance outside his domed longhouse. Voices rose in ancient song as his dark hands, webbed with wrinkles, grasped a stick and beat deer hide stretched taut across a hollow log. Drums were the heartbeat of Mother Earth. Wynonah's turtle shell rattle, alive with corn kernels, punctuated each drum beat. *Shink-shinka-shink. Shink-shinka-shink.*

One evening, Wynonah chatted endlessly about her husk doll, her leg bruise, and the berries she would pick the next day. That night, Mother sat on the corn husk mattress in the raised bench along the longhouse wall. She covered Wynonah's shoulders with a soft fur hide. Light fell from a central fire and reflected in her daughter's eyes. Mother leaned close and said, "The Great Spirit gave you two eyes, two ears, but only one mouth. Do you know why?"

Wynonah shook her head. "So you can watch and listen more than talk," Mother said tucking a strand of thick, black hair behind her daughter's ear. "Your talk tonight was a waterfall. You did not see Moon play hide-and-seek with swaying Tree branches. You did not hear Grandfather ask for Water. You did not see Brothers leave for a night hunt along the river." Wynonah felt Mother's gentle, patient guidance. "My eyes and ears will be stronger Friends," she promised.

As a child, Wynonah had vivid dreams about a tall man with red hair. "His name is Conotocarious, *Devourer of Villages*." The dreams frightened and excited her. At twelve, she went on a Vision Quest, a wilderness rite of passage. This initiation into adulthood revealed spiritual and life direction. Left alone with no food or drink on a bluff overlooking the Susquehanna, she prayed to *One Who Created Us By His Thoughts*. She asked for a Spirit Helper to guide her through Life. On the third day, an albino mink scampered up to her stillness. "Conotocarious?" she whispered to the creature with crystal eyes.

She felt its spirit was sent by The Great Mystery, the force behind Life. It would guide and protect, enabling her to fulfill obligations revealed by Creator. Her spirit was gifted with strength and humility. Thoughtful introspection became her touchstone. Destiny called.

The Long Journey of Wynonah's Lenape Delaware Ancestors

Forty thousand years ago, a landmass one thousand miles wide connected Siberia to North America. Following herds of caribou and mammoths, bands of hunters and families straggled into a glacier-covered Alaska. Over thousands of years, these ancients migrated south. Two nomadic groups, Algonquin and Iroquois, made their way east across North America.

Reaching a wide *River of Fishes*, the Mississippi, they united to defeat powerful Alligewi, who fled south leaving a river and mountain range to bear their name: Allegheny. Dividing spoils of conquest, the Iroquois claimed the Great Lakes region and tributary rivers. The Algonquin settled between the Atlantic Ocean and four great rivers: Potomac, Delaware, Hudson, Susquehanna. One Algonquin tribe, the Lenape *Original People*, lived peacefully along the Atlantic coastline in independent, family groups. They called their ancestral homeland Lenapehoking.

The Iroquois evolved into a strong Federation, destroying and absorbing neighboring tribes. Soon they set their sights on the gentle Lenape who, after being subjugated by the Iroquois, agreed to make annual payments and to never wage war, even in self-defense.

In the early 1600s, European colonists — Dutch, Swedes, English — came into this valley of enforced peace. True to their gentle nature and ever mindful of Iroquois mandates, the Lenape welcomed these pale-faced newcomers who taught them to build log houses and plow with horses and oxen. Land and pelts were traded for manufactured goods: cloth, glass, beads, blankets, horses, knives, copper/brass/iron cooking and farming tools, axes, hatchets, and guns and powder. The introduction of alcohol led to damaging abuse among natives.

In 1681, as payment for a debt of 16,000 pounds owed to Penn's admiral father, England's King Charles II granted William Penn forty-five thousand acres in the New World. Named Pennsylvania, this Lenape homeland teemed with six thousand Europeans. The great Bay was renamed Delaware along with its native peoples. Land-hungry colonists flooded inland. The sale of land to settlers by Penn's sons produced revenue to pay creditors and populate "Penn's Woods." European demand for furs, especially the soft, finely barbed underfur of the beaver, created a booming trade with the natives.

Disruption to Lenape culture was harsh. Foreign diseases killed entire tribes. Beaver became scarce. Hunting grounds shrank. Natives grew dependent on Europeans. Hunting, fishing and handicraft self-sufficiency was lost. To meet needs, Chief Sassoonan bartered more land. By the 1740s, after thousands of peaceful years in their coastal homeland, Delaware tribes were driven west to the Susquehanna River.

In boyhood, Wynonah's father, Tamaqua, fished upper Ganshowehanne (Schuylkill River) homelands with his brothers Pisquetomen and Shingas. Their venerated Grandfather Tamanend had been a wise, affable Chief. Generosity and hospitality led him to sign treaties of friendship with Europeans. He believed Great Spirit intended no one to own land, water, animals or plants. Tamanend's son Sassoonan succeeded as Chief in 1715. Sassoonan was Uncle to Pisquetomen, Tamaqua and Shingas.

"My spirit longs for the Delaware with Father Tamanend now gone many winters," Sassoonan often lamented. When Sassoonan died in 1747, many came to honor "Keeper of the Wampum." Madame Montour, a respected interpreter and political adviser, came with her grandson Shshash. Shshash was a favorite of the celebrated Algonquin-French métis granddame who lived on a Susquehanna island near Shamokin. Shshash, Lenape for *seven*, was named when he skipped a stone seven times across the Susquehanna.

In 1748, when Wynonah was 14, Shshash, who had grown into an intelligent, forthright 19-year-old brave, presented a buck and three ruffed grouse to Tamaqua, seeking permission to marry his daughter. Wynonah cherished Shshash, her childhood friend. He made her laugh and see beauty in Great Spirit's many gifts. He encouraged her to honor responsibility, cherish learning, and seek adventure. Her blood stirred with his gaze.

Shshash returns from a fishing trip on the Susquehanna.

Wynonah wove a basket and filled it with pumpkin-hickory rolls. She, Mother and Father paddled to Montour Island to present acceptance food. "I accept you, Shshash, with my gift of rolls made with nuts from hickory trees. Some tree woods are harder than hickory. Some are stronger. No other wood is gifted with both hardness and strength. You are my hickory. It is you I love." This completed the marriage. Following the Lenape matrilineal tradition of honoring lineage through the mother, Shshash moved to the bark longhouse with his wife's family.

When their first child arrived, Shshash built a separate, round wigwam. Wynonah was a loving mother. She wore a cradleboard on her back to carry

Daughter. When in the garden or cooking, she secured the board to a tree limb. Lenape rose before dawn to welcome Father Sun. Mothers held up cradleboards with dozing infants to receive rays of blessings.

From Mother, Wynonah had learned to combine herbs for cooking and how to use them for healing. Shshash hunted and fished with other braves. Meat and fish were slivered by Wynonah and placed on racks over a smoky fire to dry. Shshash burned and cleared forest land for gardens.

Only women planted crops since the Great Spirit blessed them — bearers and nurturers of Life — with the gift of fertility.

Grandmother holds Wynonah's first child in a cradleboard. A pregnant Wynonah carries a hoe after working in the garden.

15

Women's lives were full of activity — gardening, tanning, pottery, sewing, basket weaving. Cooking was done using clay, bark, stone and wood for containers and utensils. Tallow, fat from animals and plants, was collected and used to make leather dressing, soap, lubricants and candles. Women drew sap from hickory and box elder. Grinding grains and nuts into flour and meal was a daily chore. Women gathered the wood to keep fires burning, being particular about using special woods to deliver different tastes for cooking. Hunts and harvests were shared so that no one went hungry. A pot of soup always simmered on the fire. Anyone might contribute — a handful of beans, wild onions, herbs. All could smell the welcoming aroma and dip from its communal bounty.

Lenape children were loved and respected. Adult praise flowed. Patience was a gentle tool. Children were raised to be strong-willed and to think for themselves. They were not hit or humiliated. Persuasion and good example were used to instill values, integrity and confidence. Adults accepted responsibility for every child. All women were Aunts. All men were Uncles.

Elders were held in high esteem. Grandmothers took young girls foraging to collect roots, plants and flowers for food, medicine and dyeing. They gathered hemp and inner tree bark to make string and carrying bags. There was no written language, and history was preserved by word-of-mouth. It fell to female elders

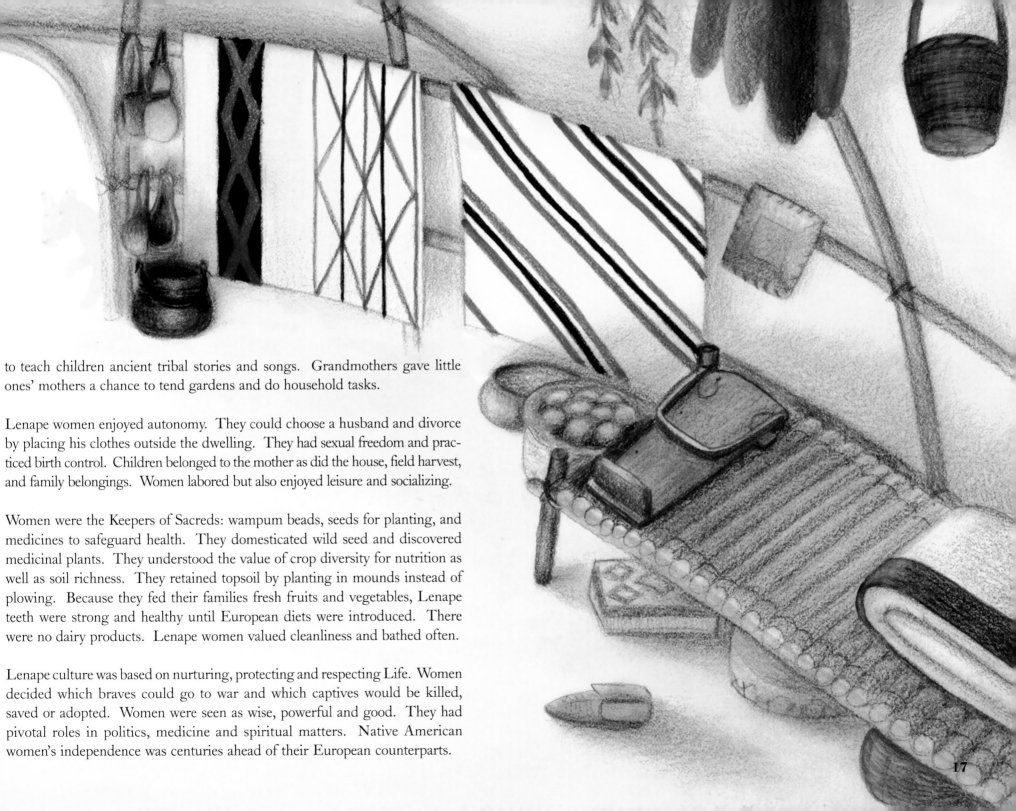

to teach children ancient tribal stories and songs. Grandmothers gave little
ones' mothers a chance to tend gardens and do household tasks.

Lenape women enjoyed autonomy. They could choose a husband and divorce
by placing his clothes outside the dwelling. They had sexual freedom and practiced birth control. Children belonged to the mother as did the house, field harvest,
and family belongings. Women labored but also enjoyed leisure and socializing.

Women were the Keepers of Sacreds: wampum beads, seeds for planting, and
medicines to safeguard health. They domesticated wild seed and discovered
medicinal plants. They understood the value of crop diversity for nutrition as
well as soil richness. They retained topsoil by planting in mounds instead of
plowing. Because they fed their families fresh fruits and vegetables, Lenape
teeth were strong and healthy until European diets were introduced. There
were no dairy products. Lenape women valued cleanliness and bathed often.

Lenape culture was based on nurturing, protecting and respecting Life. Women
decided which braves could go to war and which captives would be killed,
saved or adopted. Women were seen as wise, powerful and good. They had
pivotal roles in politics, medicine and spiritual matters. Native American
women's independence was centuries ahead of their European counterparts.

17

The Feminine Side

Giovanni da Verrazano, the first European to see Lenape, wrote in 1524: "Women are shapely and beautiful; very gracious, of attractive manner and pleasant appearance." William Penn, 160 years later, wrote that Lenape were "well built, tall and straight, strong and clever. They walk with a lofty chin." Wynonah carried herself with dignity and poise. The strength and confidence she projected enhanced her beauty. She enjoyed feminine flirtation with her husband.

Grooming

Wynonah's knee-length, blue-black hair, which she did not braid, hung loose or was rolled behind her neck. Hair was secured with hide strips decorated with bones, shells and beads. Snakeskin was used for hair bands and belts. Bear grease made hair shine. Combs were made of bone.

On occasion, red (bloodroot or pokeberry) enhancements were painted on cheeks, eyelids and ear rims; eyes were circled in black. Shell tweezers shaped eyebrows.

Dogwood branches were chewed until wood separated into a primitive toothbrush.

Cleanliness and neatness were important. Wynonah bathed daily and took steam baths in a sweat lodge several times a week. A looking glass, bartered from the English, was a handy way to check grooming.

Tattoo

Design was pricked into skin with a sharp instrument such as a fish bone. Burned poplar powder was applied. Wynonah had a seven-sided sun tattoo on her upper left arm. Animal tattoos on women were a sign of low virtue.

In 1749 Tamaqua moved his extended family west to the Kuskuskies, north of the Ohio River forks. This cluster of villages swelled with displaced natives of many tribes. Displacement caused loss of kinship structures. Religion became a mix of native beliefs and Christianity. The procession of up-rooted refugees transported Sassoonan's bones further from his Lenapehoking ancestral home. Wynonah carried family belongings in a bundle on her back. She supported its weight with a strap tumpline attached to each end of the bundle then looped around her forehead.

Summers passed. Sassoonan had designated his oldest nephew Pisquetomen to succeed as Chief. The English knew the intelligent, strong-willed Pisquetomen would be no pliant puppet and asked the Iroquois to make Shingas the Chief of all Delaware. They wanted to deal with a single "King" instead of multiple tribal Chiefs. They forced Tamaqua to stand proxy for an absent Shingas during the 1752 coronation at Logstown, 18 miles from the Ohio River forks. The English thought they could control Shingas and his "subjects" with gifts and abundant rum. That night, Wynonah took the lace crown the Iroquois had placed on her father's head and the Virginia suit of clothes they had made him wear and flung them on the fire.

French, too, sought empire. Ohio Valley control meant domination from Montreal, across the Great Lakes, down the Ohio and Mississippi, and into New Orleans. Natives had tremendous power either as an impediment or as an ally in this land thrust. Competing European nations knew dominance was impossible without the destruction or support of natives.

France advanced into the Ohio Valley. Alarmed, in 1753, Virginia sent 21-year-old George Washington to demand the French leave. A superb horseman with arms of steel, Washington had an analytical mind and a brash, confident will. His wilderness knowledge was extensive. As a teenager, he had surveyed and mapped thousands of miles of Lord Fairfax's vast Virginia holdings.

Jewelry

Wynonah wore jewelry made of beads, bone, stone, shell, glass, beaks, claws and antlers. These hung from neck, wrists and ankles. She liked small anklet bells, brass bracelets, and brass finger rings inset with glass stones. Wynonah repurposed European items such as brass thimbles and used them to decorate her clothing. Red-dyed deer hair was used for head bands, neck rings, and arm bands. She decorated clothing with beads and plant dyes. Porcupine quills were carefully woven into *lennapeuhoksen* moccasins and clothing.

Clothing

By the mid-1700s, European linen, cotton and woolen dry goods were readily available for barter. Wynonah usually draped a soft, rectangular deer pelt over a waist belt and wrapped the skirt around her legs, overlapping counterclockwise on the side. One favorite skirt was elaborately painted and decorated with porcupine quills and, from a distance, resembled lace.

Clothing was also made from beaver, raccoon, rabbit and bear skins. Hides were carefully sewn so the fur pile went down for rain runoff. Fur was used for warm bundling in winter. A warm cape, which could double as a blanket, was woven from goose or iridescent turkey feathers. Wide bands of hide were worn as thigh-calf leggings, which were attached to a belt with strips of leather. Fringe kept away insects and the leggings protected from sharp rocks, bramble, briars and snakes.

On his way to Lake Erie to present demands to the French, Washington made a courtesy visit to Chief Shingas who suggested that Virginia's Ohio Company build a strategic fort and vital trading post at the Ohio River forks. Shingas was wary of the young Virginian but pledged native allegiance. Time and again the English had made promises. Time and again natives were forced from their land. Would a permanent homeland ever be theirs? Shingas clenched his jaw and scoffed, "Will Conotocarious once again take our land?"

Washington was stunned. A century before, the first America-bound Washington had fled Cromwell's England. Great-grandfather John had married into a prosperous Virginia family, become a Burgess, church leader, court president, and military officer. He acquired Indian land through a legal trick. The displaced tribe branded him with the name Conotocarious, *Devourer of Villages*. Washington knew that natives had no written language and had preserved this name through amazing communal memory. What had enabled them to apply this genealogy across four generations? Decades later, during the Revolutionary War, Delaware natives helped in the fight for independence. They continued to call Washington "Conotocarious." He signed correspondence to them using this moniker.

Leaving Shingas, Washington continued through a treacherous winter landscape toward Lake Erie to deliver the ultimatum. France refused to relinquish its Ohio Valley claim. Exhausted, Washington headed back to Virginia. Stalked by pro-French natives, he faced down a warrior who fired a gun point-blank at his chest. The bullet veered off. Clad in native buckskin and moccasins, Washington also survived a pitch off a raft into icy Allegheny waters. Lore began to grow: the giant Conotocarious was protected by gods.

Later in September of that same year, Wynonah accompanied Father and Uncles to Carlisle, Pennsylvania to solicit help from colonials in ridding the Ohio Country of French. Rebuffed, they traveled to Winchester, Virginia where they were assured that a major summer offensive would send France running.

Being separated from her home and children was difficult for the young Lenape Mother. Wynonah was grateful she could leave them in the loving care of her mother and other tribal women.

Before leaving for Carlisle, Wynonah sliced rings of pumpkin and dangled them to dry on a long stick. "Fairy laundry webs were on grasses this morning to tell us that Father Sun will throw strong heat by midday. Wait until tomorrow to go with Grandmother and Aunts to gather nuts. Thank Brother Trees for their gifts," she reminded her children.

"As you gather nuts, Grandmother will help you create stories. Grandfather Tamaqua and I will each weave a tale as we journey. We will share story gifts when we return." She added beans and herbs to a blackened pot of simmering venison stew and stirred with a curved oak paddle Shshash had made.

Wynonah, hands dry from harvesting, dipped her fingers into a deerskin pouch of bear grease. As she rubbed the salve on her arms and hands, her son chewed golden flesh around a pumpkin stem.

Wynonah laughed and ran long fingers through his glistening black hair. "You are my Little Bear who loves pumpkin!"

20

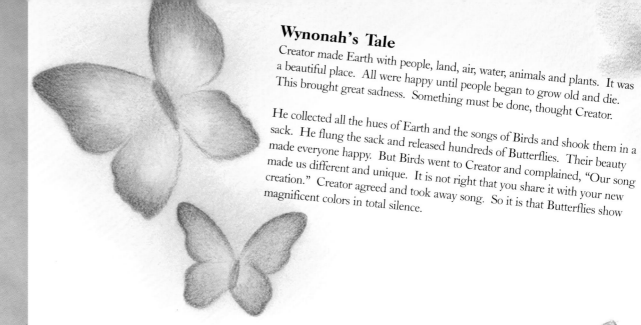

Wynonah's Tale

Creator made Earth with people, land, air, water, animals and plants. It was a beautiful place. All were happy until people began to grow old and die. This brought great sadness. Something must be done, thought Creator.

He collected all the hues of Earth and the songs of Birds and shook them in a sack. He flung the sack and released hundreds of Butterflies. Their beauty made everyone happy. But Birds went to Creator and complained, "Our song made us different and unique. It is not right that you share it with your new creation." Creator agreed and took away song. So it is that Butterflies show magnificent colors in total silence.

Tamaqua's Tale

A hunter took his bow and arrows and stalked prey for three days with no success. His family was hungry. That night he built a fire, and as he sat, he heard Owl laugh at him. This was a sign of good luck. He sprinkled a tobacco gift into the fire and spoke to Owl, asking his help.

Owl liked the strong tobacco smell and felt sorry for the hunter. "I will give you good luck with your hunt. But you must promise to hang the heart of your animal in a tree for me to eat." The hunter quickly agreed. The next day he felled a large buck, but he did not leave the heart for Owl.

Owl was angry and flew to the hunter, who carried the buck across his back. "You did not keep your promise! When you put the buck down, you will fall dead." The frightened hunter countered, "I am sorry. I worried about my family and hurried to them, forgetting my promise. I have powers, too! When you land on a branch, you will fall dead!"

Both Owl and hunter were afraid because they did not know who had the stronger power. Both became very tired, afraid to land on a branch or put down the buck. Then Owl offered, "Let us remove our curses and be good friends." And so they did. The hunter slit open the buck and hung the heart from a tree. When he got home, his wife and children celebrated with a feast.

Grandchildren's Tale

Long ago when Summer never ended, Crow had brilliant rainbow colors. Even Crow's call was beautiful. All would stop to listen when Crow sang. Then Winter came, and the people and animals were freezing. Crow was chosen to go speak to One Who Creates Things By His Thoughts. Crow would use beautiful song and ask Creator to think about Summer warmth, and it would once again be so.

Rainbow Crow flew through brittle Winter sleet to beg Creator, but Creator said he could not unthink Winter. He felt sorry for the freezing people and animals. "I will think of Fire to bring warmth!" he said. Creator plunged a long stick into Sun and gave the burning torch to Crow who flew back to Earth, hurrying before the flame burned out. Fire blackened his beautiful feathers. Smoke scorched his throat.

From that day on, Crow was a black bird with a shrill, cawing song. If you look closely, you can still see beautiful rainbow colors in Crow's black feathers.

Grandmother's Tale

In the beginning of time, there was a beautiful maiden who was a skilled weaver. She wove blankets and baskets with intricate designs and colors. Villagers from far distances would come to admire her work. She grew vain with all the praise. "I am the greatest weaver in the universe," she boasted.

Her pride did not escape notice of Creator who went to her village and challenged her to a contest. The maiden laughed as her hands flew over cloth so intricate that the villagers cheered. Creator smiled and reached into the sky, weaving swirled Clouds and a magnificent, blazing sunset. Then he wove a night sky with millions of brilliant Stars around golden harvest Moon.

The maiden knew that pride had blinded her. Ashamed, she asked Creator to forgive her. He agreed to allow her to keep her weaving skills, but he turned her into a spider, the second-best weaver in Creation.

21

Lenape Games

Lenape loved games that brought families together, taught cooperation, sharpened the senses, and built strong bodies. Races, wrestling, horseback riding, ball games, stone throws, lacrosse, hurdles, and archery were enjoyed with gusto. Competition was vigorous, but mutual respect was ever-present for all participants.

My Turtle Shell

Children each find a turtle shell and study its color and markings. Shells are put in a pile. Children line up. At a signal, they run to search for their own shell. This teaches skills of observation and awareness.

Fire Stick Guardian

Each child finds a stick as thick as a warrior's wrist and as long as his upper arm. All sit in a circle. One child is blindfolded and sticks are piled before her. Each child sneaks a stick from the pile without being grabbed by the blindfolded one. This teaches patience, body control, and listening skills.

Drum Calls

Children go to the forest and close their eyes. An elder with a drum goes to the area and occasionally beats a drum. Children keep their eyes closed and find their way to the drummer. This teaches trust, balance, coordination, and listening skills.

The following spring, Washington returned to western Pennsylvania with Virginia soldiers and allied natives. They defeated a small French brigade. Washington survived a fusillade of bullets cutting the air about his head, and natives embroidered the legend of his strong powers.

Victory was short-lived. In July, avenging French responded with a humiliating defeat of Washington's regiment at his hastily built Fort Necessity. Colonial infighting and tightened purse strings had defeated Washington as much as the French. Promised supplies and reinforcements had never arrived. Anger and frustration gnawed at his pride. Washington signed a surrender document and was allowed to retreat.

Empowered by victory, the French entrenched at Fort Duquesne and took control of the Ohio Valley. English traders fled and pro-English natives were left without a source of supplies and barter. Decades of English offenses festered in Pisquetomen, Tamaqua and Shingas. Survival was at stake. "A high wind is arising," Tamaqua told the Iroquois. In spite of dire straits, Lenape continued English support.

In 1755, the English sent a well-equipped military force, mostly Scotch and Irish, under the invincible General Edward Braddock, to crush the French. Colonel Washington headed Virginia colonials and served as Braddock's aide-de-camp.

Chief Shingas visited the arrogant, imperious Braddock whose contempt and insulting demeanor were evident. "What will happen to the land after you drive away the French?" Shingas asked. A haughty Braddock barked, "Only English will inhabit and inherit." Shingas asked if pro-English natives might live, trade and hunt on the land. "No savage should inherit land!" Braddock stormed. Shingas slashed the air with his fist. "If we have no liberty to live on the land, we will not fight!" A fool, Braddock hissed that he had no need of help from "savages" and sent them all away.

Angered with the insults and dismissive rebuff, the Lenape became silent witnesses a short distance away. Shingas, Tamaqua, Wynonah and Shshash "drew nigh the place where the engagement happened." They watched the bloody slaughter of colonials and brightly uniformed English soldiers. "Sun cuts slanting arrows through Clouds," remarked a somber Tamaqua. "It will draw Rain to wash blood from soil." French and Seneca allies put four bullets through Washington's coat and shot two horses from under him. He suffered no wounds. A Mingo warrior shouted, "Aim at someone you can kill! He is protected by Great Spirit." With Braddock near death, the young Virginia commander guided the retreat.

After this crushing English defeat, desperate natives allied themselves with the French. Pennsylvania became a bloodbath during the ensuing French and Indian War. Chief Shingas defected and became "Shingas the Terrible" as he, Pisquetomen, and Delaware and Shawnee braves raided the frontier. With French blessings and munitions, they wreaked vengeance, scalped, burned, kidnapped, and spread terror.

Hoop Games

Lenape created many games out of sticks and hoops, which might be made from vines, bones, rawhide or dried gourds. One game uses a small hoop tied by a length of hemp to the end of a stick. A player swings the hoop into the air and tries to spear it with the end of the stick. This teaches coordination and patience.

River Stones

Six flat river stones are chosen that have a dark and a light side. Stones are placed in a wide wooden bowl whose bottom is hit against the ground so stones fly up. Points are made only if stones land on all white or all black sides. This teaches that life is a game of chance and that opportunities should not be wasted.

Ball Games

Balls were made of leather, corn husks, wood, hemp, reeds, branches, stone, pods, gourds, and animal bladders. Lenape loved to play ball! Balls were hit with sticks, tossed, flung from a racket, and kicked. Two might be tied together, one moccasin apart, and then tossed to an opponent with a curved stick. Ball games teach cooperation, sharpen mental awareness, and strengthen bodies.

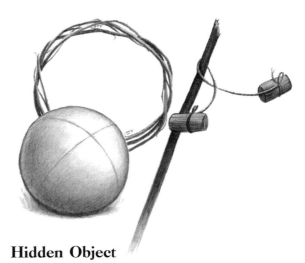

Hidden Object

Players lay moccasins in a row. One player pretends to place a small bone under each moccasin. Only one hiding place is real. Players guess which moccasin the bone is under. This teaches the skill of careful observation.

Tamaqua, named Chief after Shingas' defection, continued pursuing peace as the only hope for native autonomy. He had an even temperament and earned respect with his imposing calm. Called "King Beaver," he traveled with Wynonah to native settlements. They met with English mediators including Conrad Weiser, the Pennsylvania interpreter and diplomat who lived on the Tulpehocken, a Schuylkill River tributary where Sassoonan had once resided.

Back in the Kuskuskies, Tamaqua watched his wife bake cakes on flat stones in glowing coals. His rough hand scooped ground corn from her clay vessel. Gold meal seeped between fingers of his powerful fist. "They squeeze us from our homes. English at our backs! French toward setting sun! Iroquois to the north!"

Wynonah stoked the fire by Mother's side. She offered a corn cake spread with crushed blueberries to Father Tamaqua. She had become his "singing Heart, helping Hands, and Head with many Thoughts." Wynonah's insight and assistance were valued. Exposed to the English tongue since childhood, she had learned basic English words from her parents, expanding her vocabulary with trappers and traders. Her bilingual skill was useful both as an interpreter and astute observer. The English underestimated the high stature women held in Lenape society. Wynonah would sit unobserved as an owl in the moonlight and comprehend fully what was said when the English felt natives were out of earshot.

January
Wolf Moon

February
Snow Moon

March
Worm Moon

April
Geese Moon

May
Planting Moon

June
Strawberry Moon

Shingas defied the £20 bounty on his head and continued leading warriors in merciless retribution in Pennsylvania. In 1756, colonials burned the Allegheny River town of Kittanning, the largest Delaware settlement and Shingas' home base. Its destruction crippled native assaults and shocked them into seeing their mission's futility. Was it time to bury the *tamahikan* tomahawk?

Tamaqua saw the Kittanning setback as an opportunity for peace. He sent Pisquetomen and Wynonah east to "know the truth of affairs." The crown promised natives peace and protection on land west of the Allegheny Mountains if they would cease their support of France. In a final showdown, British General John Forbes would lead an expedition to the Ohio forks.

In October 1758, a weary Tamaqua was hopeful of an English victory and conveyance of Ohio lands to natives. His voice shook with emotion as he proclaimed, "The land is ours!" He mandated, "All Indians from sunrise to sunset should join the peace." Shingas, granted immunity in exchange for cessation of native attacks, stood by his brother's side. King Beaver Tamaqua and twelve other Indian chiefs agreed to the Treaty of Easton, pledging full support of the British in exchange for "peace and protection west of the mountains." Wynonah helped make white wampum belts to present as a sign of peace.

Two hundred miles to the south, Wynonah's partner in Destiny was busy with important personal matters.

Shaman *Powwawn* Healer*

Shaman healers served as mediums to the spirit world. Power came from Creator. Shamans possessed skill and common sense. They used prayer, ceremonies, songs, magic, exhortation, herbs and medicines. Shamans practiced sweating, poulticing, massage, bone setting, and body manipulation. Good health meant harmony and balance between the body, mind, spirit, fellow beings, and nature. Shamans assisted in childbirth and were present for the dying. They were highly respected.

Bear Grease	salve, sun and wind protection	Wild Cherry	general tonic, cough
Butterfly Weed	pleurisy	Cone Flower	venereal disease
May Apple, Dandelion	laxative	Ragweed	blood poison
Black Walnut	remove bile	Bayberry, Wintergreen	kidney ailments
Tobacco, Elm, Pine	burns, scalds	Wild Carrot	diabetes
Onions	induce lactation, cold syrup	Yarrow	liver and kidney disorders
Sassafras	rheumatism, reduce fever	Willow Bark (aspirin)	aches and pains
Sycamore, Oak	sore throat, cough, hoarseness	Prickly Ash	heart problems
Redbud	reduce fever, stop vomiting	Cattail	kidney stones
Dogwood	tonic	Bittersweet	salve, clear up liver spots
Spider Webs	suture; applied to wounds	Pin Oak	intestinal pain
Ginger, Milkweed, Sage	birth control	Skunk Cabbage	whooping cough, epilepsy
Sumac	sores and skin eruptions	Milkweed	epilepsy
Turnip, Blackberry	diarrhea, dysentery	White Pine	scurvy
Goldenrod	diarrhea, reduce fever	Blue Flag Iris	gallstones

Different parts — root, stem, leaf, flower — of plants were used.
*Use caution with native medicines, which may be toxic. No recommendations are implied.

July
Buck Moon

August
Sturgeon Moon

September
Harvest Moon

October
Hunter Moon

November
Beaver Moon

December
Long Night Moon

25

Wynonah's Larder*

Meat and Fish

Deer, bear, beaver, elk, rabbit, squirrel, turkey, raccoon, muskrat, porcupine, pigeon, grouse, goose, duck, snail, frog, turtle, mussel, crayfish, bass, bluegill, sunfish, pike, perch, pickerel, snake, eggs of birds and fowl, insects such as locust.

Vegetables, Fruits and Nuts

Squash, pumpkin, corn, beans, peas, sorrel, onion, watercress, cattail root, dandelion, milkweed, mushrooms, poke. Grapes, plums, crab apples, huckleberry, strawberry, blackberry, gooseberry, raspberry, thimbleberry, blueberry, elderberry, red cedar berry. Chestnuts, hickory nuts, hazelnuts, beech nuts, walnuts, butternuts. Acorns for flour.

Beverages

"Coffee" from roasted chicory root, corn, sunflower seeds, burnt dandelion root. Tea from sassafras root, wintergreen, evergreen needles, cherry bark/twigs. Nut milk from mashed, boiled, strained nut meats. "Lemonade" from boiled staghorn sumac red fruit clusters.

Herbs and Sweeteners

Allspice, wild mint, sweet bay, mustard. Tapped maple, honey, green corn stalk sap, wild grapes, and berry juice. Salt was not used.

Cooking Methods

Most cooking was done over an open fire. Liquids were also boiled by dropping in hot stones. Iron kettles, knives and utensils were traded from Europeans. Meat and fish might be wrapped in mud and baked over hot coals. Open-rack smoking cured meat and fish.

Food Storage

Smoked and dried meat and fish strips could last a year. Food was smoked over a pit for several days to acquire a delicious taste and keep away insects and animals. Pits were dug and lined with bark for storing root vegetables and nuts. Vegetables, fruits and berries were sun dried or placed near a fire. Animal fats were stored in clay pots and rawhide pouches.

*Use caution ingesting native foods. No recommendations are implied.

Wynonah's Wedding Gift
Pumpkin-Hickory Rolls

Roast pumpkin over coals. Cool, peel, then mash.
Grind corn into meal.
Hull, chop and roast hickory nuts.
Mix two scoops of corn to one scoop of nut meal. Add pumpkin and honey to moisten. Shape into balls two fingers thick. Wrap in green corn shucks, and tie with hemp.
Drop into boiling water for 10-15 minutes.

George Washington was in love.

He left the estate of Martha Custis after securing her promise to marry when his military duties ended at year's end. Guiding his steed off the Pamunkey River ferry, he headed toward his post at Winchester, Virginia. His newly betrothed walked in the garden of her 21,000 acre Virginia estate. The wealthy widow had said "yes" to the handsome 26-year-old Colonel.

At six feet two, George towered over most men. He had an extraordinary physique: long arms and legs, large feet and hands. His face had a calm majesty: wide, clenched mouth; broad nose with scattered pockmarks from a bout with smallpox; blue-gray eyes in deep sockets; a shock of reddish hair pulled behind in a queue.

He would be Martha's perfect companion, father to her two children, and a gentleman farmer. Martha worried about George's approaching military campaign with General Forbes. George had twice failed to drive France out of western Pennsylvania and the Ohio Country. Soon he would again lead Virginia troops to join other colonials on their march to Fort Duquesne.

Martha had sewn a linen shirt for George to wear under his woolen uniform. Brass shank buttons with amethyst stones secured the cuffs and front lapels. "To keep you warm and safe, my Love."

27

Tamaqua had told Wynonah about Conotocarious-Washington. "He is a sapling, full of wild energy with strength and daring of many warriors. He walks in your dreams as a great leader who helps our people. At Fort Necessity, his Lenape guide, Maehhumund, told him of albino mink in the land of our Lehigh Brothers. This Virginia warrior has pledged his heart and wants a fine coat for his bride."

Tamaqua, his hands on Wynonah's shoulders, chose his words with earnest deliberation. "Sassoonan's spirit longs for his Father Tamanend. Go find Conotocarious. Persuade him to travel with you to take Sassoonan's bones to old hunting grounds on Ganshowehanne near Bear Creek where ancients camped. Here Sassoonan's spirit can flow to Tamanend who sleeps eternally near the Delaware. It must be Conotocarious who helps bury the bones so ancients will bind him as a Lenape Brother with gifts of wisdom, strength, courage. Promise Conotocarious the albino pelts and safe escort to Virginia."

British military constructed a corduroy road of cleared trees into western Pennsylvania. Soldiers, wagons, cannon, munitions, supplies, horses and cattle cut through the wilderness. Washington commanded Virginia troops under Forbes. In November 1758, after bloody years of fighting, the English found Fort Duquesne deserted and burned by the fleeing French.

Forbes left colonials to guard the newly named Fort Pitt. Washington hastened south to Loyalhanna, now called Fort Ligonier, and detailed a courier for crucial supplies. It was early December. Grateful for unseasonably warm weather, he opened his uniform jacket. Feeling the soft linen of Martha's handmade shirt, roughened fingers idly flicked the brass buttons. His military commission was over. He could wed Martha and return to make their home in his beloved Mount Vernon.

Raising his spyglass toward trees at fort's edge, George recognized Maehhumund, a Delaware ally at Fort Necessity. With him was a stately female native with a lofty chin. She met his gaze with dignity and grace. The native pair dismounted and approached on foot.

"Conotocarious sees into forest with spyglass," she mused as she stood before her dream walker. "Can you see into our hearts?" Wynonah studied the pale Colonel. She felt *manito* power of her Spirit Being that would enable her to achieve stability for her people. Her bones and flesh were part of a bigger world — Wind, Stars, Trees, Mountains, Rivers.

Wynonah spoke to the tall Virginian. "A welcome peace settles across the land, gifted to all by Great Spirit. My Father, Chief Tamaqua, asks me to guide your path to mink pelts white as snow."

George glanced at the natives' horses and touched a blanket-wrapped bundle. Wynonah placed a protective hand on the bundle's cinched cord. "It is yet to be. First we must travel to Ganshowehanne, in your tongue, Schuylkill River. The way is long, the wind grows cold. Corn Mother made husks thick this harvest. Winter will have sharp teeth and come soon. Lenape will keep safe our journey. Lehigh Brothers will bring pelts."

George was puzzled. "Ask Lehigh natives to come here. I will pay for pelts."

"We barter for things greater than pelts, worth more than coins." Wynonah told him of the Lenape sacred need to bury Sassoonan's bones where his spirit could flow down to the Delaware.

George gaped and then did something sorely missing in recent months. He threw back his head and filled the air with laughter. "And why not?" he thought. "My troops are secure. Supplies will soon arrive. I am free of military duties. One more adventure before settling down to farming might be just what I need." He imagined Martha wrapped in white fur. "I will do as you ask!"

Love and Destiny are forces that distort Time, upend Logic, and change History.

George and Wynonah made their way east across the Raystown Path. She deftly led and did not hesitate to ford streams, jump fallen trees, or guide them safely along narrow, mountain ridges. *Clip-clop, clip-clop, clip-clop.* Her ears were attentive to the hoof beats of her companion's horse.

"Your mouth curls like a smile with a secret," she said after they had climbed a steep gorge.

"We could have won the war years ago if you had led our troops over these dense mountains," he replied.

"Ah!" Wynonah laughed. "Then yours was a smile of respect?"

"Respect? Yes, and curiosity," George answered. "How is it that a woman can do such things? You have unusual skill, strength and bravery."

"Such women are not rare if allowed to reach for Father Sun and flourish in Mother Earth. Should women have still hands, empty minds, dull spirits?" she retorted. Wynonah spoke of the respect held by women in Lenape villages.

Miles fell behind. Wynonah told of Shshash, her children, and her hope of living without fear and continued eviction. George opened to the warmth of his noble Lenape companion. Normally reticent and guardedly private, he shared stories of his setbacks and triumphs, friends and family, hopes and dreams.

He told her of his mother Mary's letter to him in the midst of the frontier war with France. "She was out of butter and demanded that I immediately get her some!" They both swayed in their saddles, laughing heartily. "She loves to stay on her farm near Fredericksburg. All she needs is her rocking chair on the porch, tobacco for her pipe, and the family Bible."

"And butter!" Wynonah reminded him.

"When I was 14, my belongings were already on ship, and I was set to board a man-of-war in the Potomac. Mother forbade me to join England's navy. She doesn't approve of my life as a soldier either. Soon I will return to Virginia to farm my land. That will please her."

They rode in comfortable companionship. "Mother is famous all over Virginia for her gingerbread," the weary soldier shared.

Details of their journey burned into George's memory.

Changes of exhausted horses . . . Maehhumund emerging from dense forests with supply-laden natives . . . warming fires, prepared food . . . travel through water and wind gaps. George, at times in stuporous slumber, progressed north-east day and night. By his side rode the erect Lenape squaw, black hair rolled at her nape, a sacred bundle of bones across her saddleless horse.

The weary pair stopped north of *endless hill* Kittatinny Blue Mountain. Before them stood Fort Lebanon, a 100-by-100 foot stockade. George approached an entry door in the 14-foot high walls and called out. The fort was used by 40 area families as a refuge from marauding natives. It was deserted.

The nearby Schuylkill River, fed by rushing mountain brooks, meandered and turned, at times flowing in a northerly direction back toward its source before gliding southeast to the Delaware Bay. On its oxbow bend near Bear Creek, George and Wynonah prepared Sassoonan for his final journey.

Chants, wails and low drum beats drifted from riverside mountain laurel and rock ledges. George wondered how many natives kept vigil that cold December night. *Shink-shinka-shink. Shink-shinka-shink.*

Before daybreak, promised pelts white as snow were secured to a fresh horse. Corn cakes sizzled on flat stones in a glowing fire. Wynonah turned brook trout skewered on long sticks. "Mary's bread of ginger would taste good with Brother Fish," she mused.

"Yes," laughed George. "Perhaps we should send her a request demanding a pan of warm gingerbread this instant!"

George drank from a crystal Schuylkill. Wild turkey caught his attention and black-capped chickadees announced their presence — *tsick-dee-dee-dee* — from bushy hemlock. When a mountain lion's cry carried down the valley, George gripped his rifle, which rested near his side.

"As boys, Father and Uncles speared fish here," Wynonah said. "From Tamaqua I learned to snare fish. It is sad your father died when you were small." She handed him a turtle shell bowl filled with smashed sassafras root and water. Heated pebbles hissed and perfumed the air as she dropped them in.

"I've had many fathers," said George while sipping hot brew. He scooped a piece of trout, and his tongue savored warm flakes of the river's bounty.

Triangular pieces of brass, rolled up and secured to legging thongs, jingled when Wynonah moved. A beaver skin robe clung to her long frame as she squatted on moccasins decorated with beads and porcupine quills. Around her neck

hung a string of white wampum beads. From the middle dangled a brownish-red turtle totem carved from catlinite. Lenape believed the world was created on the back of a giant turtle that rose out of the ocean.

Sharing a crusty corn cake with George, she stood, brushing crumbs from her lap. "My heart is happy to feel you as Brother. All Delaware wish to live with friendship such as we have woven." Her breath curled into the cold morning air.

They mounted neighing horses, and the return journey began. Cresting a ridge, they made their way down and crossed Plum Creek. George turned to see a glorious sunrise when his horse slipped, pitching its rider into a thicket of alder.

"George Washington! George Washington!" cried Wynonah. Dismounting, she rolled the listless equestrian to his back. Brushing back his red hair, she saw a welt across his temple. George moaned. Blood seeped from under his great coat. "Be still!" she commanded. Stripping his coat, she took sharpened quartz from a pouch hung about her waist and cut away the linen shirt. A gash along his collarbone was treated with a poultice of Plum Creek water, primrose oil, and turkey down, then covered with strips of linen shirt. A competent shaman healer, concern reflected from Wynonah's hazel eyes.

They sat near Plum Creek until George convinced her he was fine. With native help, the journey continued through Pine Grove, across the Allegheny Path near Harris' Ferry, down the Virginia Path through Maryland, and into Virginia.

"It is time, Brother, to say good-bye." Wynonah took George's hand and placed white wampum beads in his palm. "This I know. You will lead a powerful nation when it is but a seed. Often will come great winds, little rain, thunder feet. You must help the seed sprout like a vine, grow strong like an oak. You must also be just and wise with my Sisters and Brothers so we, too, have a home." Her fingers closed around his. He felt the beads as she squeezed his fist chanting, "Oh, Wisdom. Oh, Strength. Oh, Courage. Oh, Knowledge. Oh, Love. Go with Brother George. Guide his feet and his heart."

Wynonah turned to remount. "Wait!" George called out. He placed his spyglass across her lap. The two parted. Wynonah turned her horse and headed north. George arrived in Winchester on December 8, 1758.

George

The next month, January 1759, Washington wore a suit of blue and silver with red trimmings and gold knee buckles at his wedding. As his bride rode in the carriage to Mount Vernon, she tapped her purple silk shoes and felt the warmth of her husband's wedding gift, a mink coat of the purest white.

For 17 years, Washington farmed, managed their vast estate, served on the House of Burgess, and felt the changing tide of relations with England. In 1774 he was a delegate to the first Continental Congress. When the colonies declared independence, he accepted command of the Continental Army. Freedom's fight was long and difficult. Once more, Washington was hampered with colonial infighting, lack of funds, and insufficient recruits. Victory seemed impossible. Washington's strong will, character, and common sense inspired the fledgling nation.

In the war's darkest hour, surrounded by 32,000 British, an exhausted Washington examined maps of Long Island. Fingers rolled white beads in his uniform pocket as he walked to his bed chamber tent. Rest was needed before evacuating his massive army that August 1776 night. His aide-de-camp, Pennsylvania's Thomas Mifflin, glanced at scribbles on the map's edge: *Win, When, Wyn-o-nah-Whenona?* "The General thinks of victory," Mifflin said, erasing all but a positive prophecy: *Win!* Evading the enemy, Washington went on to deliver brilliant blows to the British, securing victory and independence.

Yet again, in 1789 Washington answered the call of duty and served, over Martha's strong objection, as the nation's first President. In 1797, the Father of His Country retired to his beloved Mount Vernon. In December 1799 he trotted on horseback in his blue great coat, blue overalls, and bespattered boots to inspect his fields. As he rode through freezing rain he thought back, as he often did, to that December journey four decades earlier. What happened to her? Was she alive? The cold brought an ache to his collarbone. He smiled, knowing the scar there was the only one on a body that had spent much of its life in battle.

Struggle for land continued with natives. During the Revolutionary War, Indians served as scouts and guides for colonial troops. In 1778 Congress dealt a crushing blow by refusing to ratify a treaty that would have made Ohio Indian Territory the 14th state. In retirement, George hoped to find a way to establish an Indian state. To that end, he had begun drafting a proposal, "A Home State of Their Own," that he hoped Jefferson would redress with Congress. In his pocket, he fingered ever-present, white wampum beads. "For Wynonah!" he shouted, the words freezing in crisp air.

Two days later, at the age of 67, the great leader's chest heaved with pneumonia, and he lost his final fight. Martha buried her husband at Mount Vernon. With tender care, she put the wampum beads over his heart and placed his great hands over their whiteness. She joined him two years later.

Wynonah

Shshash greeted his wife as she returned to the Kuskuskies. She snuggled with her children around a crackling fire and told them of her journey with Conotocarious. Mother ladled warm squirrel stew. Shshash knelt behind and rubbed his wife's shoulders with his broad hands. "Sassoonan is at rest," said Tamaqua. "Where will our spirits find a home?"

The next day, Wynonah took linen shirt remains from her pouch. She cut off brass shank buttons. Amethyst stones reflected deep purple in the sunlight. "Come, Daughter," she called to her eldest. They restrung her necklace with alternating buttons and wampum beads, placing the small turtle in its central spot. Wynonah watched Daughter try it on and primp in a looking glass. Then Wynonah placed it around her own neck.

The following summer 1759, Tamaqua led Delaware, Shawnee and Wyondots and went with Pisquetomen, Wynonah and Shshash to Fort Pitt to meet with the British to re-establish trade and hunting. The Lenape King Beaver was dedicated to peace and respected as a Grandfather Sachem leader. Peace was fragile and unstable as young warriors like Pontiac ascended.

Before moving his family to Tuscarawas in Ohio, Tamaqua wanted one last trip to his childhood hunting grounds. Guided by Wynonah, they went to Sassoonan's burial place. Near the edge of Plum Creek, Wynonah wrapped the spyglass and her necklace in a soft pelt. Tamaqua dug a hole where his daughter placed her cherished bundle. They planted a red maple sapling and tapped the earth around the edges of their peace offering to the Ages.

In 1761, Seneca black wampum belts were passed to enlist all natives in a united war. The three Lenape Brothers hurled their belts against the wall. Treaty of Easton promises were dust in the wind. Europeans surged into native lands in the Ohio Country. Shingas was gravely ill. Pisquetomen died in 1762. The peace he and Tamaqua had worked hard to build crumbled. A broken man in spirit and health, Tamaqua could do little but watch natives and English inflict pain. In 1771 King Beaver Tamaqua's spirit journeyed to his brothers and Sassoonan.

A year later, Wynonah learned that Conotocarious, now 38, was to travel to Fort Pitt and go by canoe to the junction of the Ohio and Kanawha Rivers. He would leave his affairs at Mount Vernon to survey lands promised to Virginia troops as payment for service. The Lenape Princess was 36, a Grandmother, and a respected shaman. She traveled to the Kanawha. Overhead, geese flew low in a disorganized zag, foretelling an approaching storm. Wynonah's hazel eyes watched the middle-aged man, hair graying at the temples, who rhythmically dipped his paddle into strong current. He did not see the lone figure who stood tall on the shore.

— Epilogue —
Generations Later

Sunshine streamed through the mullioned windows in the log cabin. Mother looked out over Lake Wynonah's diamond sparkle. She felt the glow of inner contentment.

In 1970, a dam had been built across Plum Creek. Water filled the valley with pristine beauty. The lake was named after Wynonah, a remarkable Lenape Delaware woman.

Children laughed and splashed at lake's edge. Mother folded blueberries into golden cornbread batter. Soon the sweet smell of muffins filled the summer kitchen.

"Mommy! Look what we found!" Maisie ran into the house with Luke close behind. "We were digging near the red maple tree!" Maisie held brass buttons with purple centers, small white beads, and a tiny carved turtle. Luke put the found treasures in soapy water while Mother got string.

"These are beautiful! Let's make a necklace for Maisie!" Mother exclaimed. "I wonder how the buttons, beads and turtle got here."

The spyglass has never been found.

41

Buttons & Beads

is set in Caslon typeface, which was designed in London in the early 1700s. This robust serif font was to be used in religious tracts that would teach Christianity to natives in the New World. Caslon, the favored type for colonial printers, was used in the Declaration of Independence and the Constitution.

Referenced Works

Bruchac, James and Joseph 2000 *Native American Games and Stories*. Fulcrum Publishing, Golden, CO.

Burke, Francis 1971 *An Archaic Site in Schuylkill County, Pennsylvania*. Historical Society of Orwigsburg, Orwigsburg, PA.

Densmore, Frances 1974 *How Indians Use Wild Plants for Food, Medicine and Crafts*. Dover Publications, New York, NY.

Donehoo, George 2006 *A History of the Indian Villages and Place Names in Pennsylvania*. Wennawoods Publishing, Lewisburg, PA.

Flexner, James 1965 *George Washington: The Forge of Experience*. Little Brown, Boston, MA.

Grumet, Robert 1996 *Northeastern Indian Lives 1632-1816*. University of Massachusetts Press, Amherst, MA.

Hirsch, Allison Duncan 2004 "Indian, Métis, and Euro-American Women on Multiple Frontiers" from *Friends and Enemies in Penn's Woods*. The Pennsylvania State University Press, University Park, PA.

Isely, Bliss 1962 *The Horseman of the Shenandoah*. Bruce Publishing, Milwaukee, WI.

Jennings, Francis 1988 *Empire of Fortune*. Norton & Co., New York, NY.

Kalman, Bobbie 2001 Life in a Longhouse Village. Crabtree Publishing, New York, NY.

Kent, Barry 1994 *Discovering Pennsylvania's Archeological Heritage*. Commonwealth of Pa., Harrisburg, PA.

Kraft, Herbert 2001 *The Lenape-Delaware Indian Heritage*. Lenape Books, Stanhope, NJ.

Kraft, Herbert 2005 *The Lenape or Delaware Indians*. Lenape Lifeways, Inc., Stanhope, NJ.

Maxwell, James 1995 *America's Fascinating Indian Heritage*. Reader's Digest, Pleasantville, NY.

Nolan, J. Bennett 1951 *The Schuylkill*. Rutgers University Press, New Brunswick, NJ.

Porter, Eliot 1973 *Appalachian Wilderness*. Ballantine Books, New York, NY.

Sipe, C. Hale 1927 *The Indian Chiefs of Pennsylvania*. Wennawoods Publishing, Lewisburg, PA.

Steer, Diana 1996 *Native American Women*. Barnes & Noble, New York.

Tantaquidgeon, Gladys 1972 *Folk Medicine of the Delaware and Related Algonkian Indians*. Commonwealth of Pa., Harrisburg, PA.

Wallace, Paul 1965 *Indian Paths of Pennsylvania*. Commonwealth of Pa., Harrisburg, PA.

Wallace, Paul 1981 *Indians in Pennsylvania*. Commonwealth of Pa., Harrisburg, PA.

Wenning, Scott 2000 *Handbook of the Delaware Indian Language*. Wennawoods Publishing, Lewisburg, PA.

Weslager, C. A. 1972 *The Delaware Indians: A History*. Rutgers University, New Brunswick, NJ.

Wilbur, Keith 1995 *The Woodland Indians*. The Globe Pequot Press, Guilford, CT.

Williams, Toni 2000 *50 Birds and Mammals of Pennsylvania*. Pennsylvania Game Commission, Harrisburg, PA.

Note: The internet is a rich source of Lenape Delaware, American Indian information.

Gretchen E. Hardy

When Gretchen moved to Lake Wynonah in 2000, she wanted to learn more about the history of the area especially the natives who had shared this awesome land of tranquility and beauty. Information was scant. She also wondered about Wynonah. Who was she, how did she survive, what made her laugh/think/cry/sing/strive? Was she more of a *Sister* than a voiceless ancient who disappeared into history? Years of research began. *Buttons & Beads* tells the story of the land and Wynonah. Gretchen holds a degree in journalism from Kent State University and has done graduate work in marketing and psychology at Penn State University. This is her third published book. She enjoys family, landscaping, felting, snowshoeing, collecting oxymorons, and sipping a mug of hot tea on the dock in Lake Wynonah. She and her husband, Richard, live lakeside in a log home dwarfed by a giant red maple.

Zoungy Kligge

Zoungy drew his first picture (of a backhoe) at age 18 months and has been creating art ever since. He earned a bachelor's degree in sculpture from Rhode Island School of Design, although one of his favorite classes was writing and illustrating for children. In 2009, Gretchen invited him to illustrate *Buttons & Beads*. Months of research were devoted to the imagery to achieve the best possible historical accuracy. This included details as small as George Washington's handwriting style, and the species of fish Wynonah most likely would have caught in December 1758 on the Schuylkill River. Zoungy has worked with 3D computer graphics as well and spent six summers teaching at Appel Farm Arts Camp in Elmer, New Jersey. He lives in Pennsylvania. *Buttons & Beads* is his first published illustrated book.

With Grateful Appreciation

For the encouragement of my incredible husband, Richard, the fulcrum of my life,

the creative genius of Zoungy Kligge,

research enthusiasm from Fred Kligge,

the Lake Wynonah Book Group,

Dr. Courtney McKay Stevens,

Barbara Stopp, and

David and Bonnie Tyson.

Proceeds from the sale of Buttons & Beads will be donated to the Lake Wynonah Civic Association, Auburn, Pennsylvania.